Sweet the Moments

Reflections for Women on Everyday Things

DeLyn Davis Wagenknecht

NORTHWESTERN PUBLISHING HOUSE
Milwaukee, Wisconsin

Library of Congress Control Number: 2002100792
Northwestern Publishing House
1250 N. 113th St., Milwaukee, WI 53226-3284
http://www.nph.net
© 2002 Northwestern Publishing House
Published 2002
Printed in the United States of America
ISBN 978-0-8100-1469-5

For my mother, Evelyn K. Davis;
mother-in-law, Marcella Wagenknecht;
mentors Judy Zahn and Carolyn Cunningham;
and Rev. Robert F. Ingram,
who made me think.

Contents

Foreword

In God's eyes I am significant. So are you. Each moment of our lives, no matter how mundane or annoying, has significance—for us and for the other people in our lives. Every second can show us something about ourselves as God's children. There is no moment that is not known to him. He has ordained the moments of our lives; he is in control of each one. We can use even the most insignificant of them to become more powerful, more faithful, and more joyful.

The apostle Paul encourages us to think about things that are *noble, praiseworthy,* and *excellent* (Philippians 4:8). I often find it difficult to think about these things of God during trying and tedious times. Yet, looking at these moments in retrospect through the filter of Scripture, with an eye for the Lord's strength (and sometimes with a sense of humor), I learn much about who I am and what God wants me to become.

When I was in high school the youth minister of our church liked to play mentally challenging games during youth group outings. One of the games was designed to make us stop and take note of the spiritual importance of the things we were doing at one exact moment. We called the game *significant moments.* While we were riding in a van, eating at a fast-food restaurant, skating at a skating rink, or just sitting around talking at Bible camp; our counselor would ask, "What is the spiritual significance of this moment?" We would then respond with answers that showed how we understood that particular situation to have meaning in our Christian lives. The game kept our minds focused on God and his grace. *And* it was fun.

I have played this game with myself for many years. I still enjoy it, and I still discover new insights each time I play. Sometimes I record the story of the moment, shaping it into a narrative or, occasionally, a poem. Each entry takes me to a particular Bible text that has had special meaning for me, and each text often leads me to say a prayer. Over the years I have gathered a small collection of these moments of spiritual significance. I hope you enjoy reading some of them. Perhaps you'll even join me in playing the game of *significant moments*.

Editor's Preface

For Martin Luther the female perspective was deserving of great admiration. "Earth has nothing more tender," he wrote, "than a woman's heart when it is the abode of piety."

How remarkably true and wise! Women perceive life in a way that is profoundly different from a man's understanding. Sometimes the differences are subtle. At other times a woman's viewpoint stands in bold juxtaposition to a male's view. Subtle or stark, a woman's view on life is inevitably unique because it uses the human heart as its filter.

This book is part of an effort to give voice to the expressions of godly women in every walk and stage of life. The purpose of this book and others like it is to examine the great themes and important struggles that are part of every Christian woman's experience—to help her explore her blessings, examine her faith, inspire her family, endure her suffering, excel in her prayer life, and become fully engaged in the worship of her Savior-God.

In a world gone giddy with the ideology of radical feminism, these books written by women and for women provide a meaningful dialogue bathed in the light of God's eternal Word. May the give and take of these timeless conversations bring glory to God's holy name and a rich harvest of blessings to this book's readers.

Kenneth J. Kremer, editor

I can do everything through him who gives
me strength.

Philippians 4:13

Forbid it, Lord, that I should boast
Save in the death of Christ, my God.
All the vain things that charm me most,
I sacrifice them to his blood.

Christian Worship [CW] *125:2*

Fear and Pride

I didn't think I could do it. With all of my might, I was wishing that I could just get up and walk out of the room. It was my first literary conference. I was scheduled to read my own paper. A crowd of English professors and graduate students from all over the country had filed into the conference room to hear what I had to say about one of my favorite women authors. I wore a new blue suit with new shoes to match. I had new stockings (without any runs). I had a paper approved by my professor. And I had a bad case of butterflies. The speaker who occupied the podium before me droned on. I tried to listen, but my ears were ringing and hot—I was petrified.

Then, over the ringing in my ears, I heard my name announced as I was introduced to speak. I said a silent prayer—something to the effect that if it was God's will, I would survive this ordeal. On the way to the podium I added a prayer of thanks that the distance between my chair and the podium was not great. I wasn't sure I could have walked much farther. I was convinced that, given a few more steps, my new blue shoes would make me trip. They didn't.

When I arrived at the podium, my ears stopped ringing, and a new sensation of peace and tranquility washed over me. I was surprised to find myself suspended in such a relaxed frame of mind. "Maybe this isn't going to be so difficult," I thought. After all, the hard work had already been done. My paper was right in front of me. All I had to do was read it, just as I had rehearsed it a hundred times before.

I began to read, pretending that I was the only person in the room. My voice got stronger as I went along, and then I was done.

When I finished reading the paper, I breathed a quiet sigh of relief, thinking I was home free. But I wasn't.

A woman raised her hand and asked a question. This wasn't just any woman either. She was widely recognized as *the* authority in the field of Restoration Drama. I had quoted her in my paper. "Oh, dear God," I pleaded, "please, help me!" Again, as I muttered the prayer to myself, a strange sense of calm came over me. The answer that tumbled out came as such a measured, articulate response that it surprised me even as I spoke. Even more surprising was the fact that the woman nodded in agreement, and then said to the whole assembly that she agreed with me. Oh, happy day!

It didn't take long for me to forget how God had answered my prayers and to start congratulating myself for being so insightful, so observant, so elegant in my logic, and so articulate in expressing my literary understanding in such profound rhetoric.

Then, just as I was feeling much too pleased with myself, one of my classmates invited me to accompany her to another conference room to hear another paper. In an instant my grand moment was gone. This other paper was brilliant. There were a lot of very smart people there to probe the author's thesis with intelligent questions. And the answers that the essayist gave were gems of careful, thought-provoking ideas aimed at stimulating the intellect of this academic crowd. Then it was time to go home.

At the end of the day, I was alone again, just myself and my God. I was no longer afraid, nor was I any longer full of my own brilliance. I was just grateful; God had given what I needed in my moment—self-confidence, liberally seasoned with some well-deserved humility. He had gotten me through the day. With his help I had done well. Perhaps someday I would become a professor of English. But for now, as the day ended, I was content with being a student and a happy child of God. I knew that he would be with me in my future, wherever that would lead. After all, he had already done the most difficult and most important work for me. God had forgiven my sins, given me hope in his promise of eternal life, and provided a purpose for my life and the necessary gifts to live it in his service. What more could I want?

Whether my future led me to become a professional instructor or a professional mom, or something I had not yet dreamed of, I would live my life to the glory of Jesus' name. I would lean on him—my strength and my salvation.

If my people, who are called by my name, will humble themselves and pray and seek my face and turn from their wicked ways, then will I hear from heaven and will forgive their sin and will heal their land.

2 Chronicles 7:14

The LORD has heard my cry for mercy;
the LORD accepts my prayer.

Psalm 6:9

A Letter to My Best Friend from Bible Camp

I stand here by the lake near our old Bible camp, alone now, just me and my feelings and doubts—the same feelings and doubts you and I used to share. Everyone else here seems to have it all together. I remember every moment we spent here. I hold this place as a child holds a teddy bear, never wanting to let go of the love the Lord showed me here.

> As I sit here sulking a bit, I hear a sound
> As though someone has opened a floodgate on the other side
>   of the lake.
> I see something far away
> That looks like steam rising from hot pavement.
> It is the beating of a hundred pairs of wings,
> Propelling ducks low over the water.
> Nothing that I do could ever be this beautiful.
> Nowhere that I go could ever be as perfect as this place.

My life is a lot like this lake. I'm a good camp counselor. My faith seems smooth on the surface; others can see Jesus reflected in me. But under the surface are the weeds and the mud of my old self. Even you, my dear friend, cannot see what is there. These are the sins I hide and keep only to myself. Only the Lord is able to seek them out, though I try to keep him from diving too deep.

Every ripple hurts.
Every weed pulled by him is a miracle
That lets my thoughts flow easier
As the guilt and the pain fly away on the wings of the ducks.

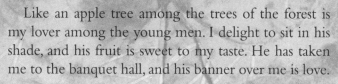

Like an apple tree among the trees of the forest is my lover among the young men. I delight to sit in his shade, and his fruit is sweet to my taste. He has taken me to the banquet hall, and his banner over me is love.

Song of Songs 2:3, 4

I will betroth you to me forever; I will betroth you in righteousness and justice, in love and compassion. I will betroth you in faithfulness, and you will acknowledge the LORD.

Hosea 2:19, 20

Prince Charming, at Last

I am sliding down the aisle
In Cinderella slippers.
You are standing, smiling, next to me.
In all the years of dreams and nightmares,
I never thought that this could be.

I give you my flowers
And take his hand
And look into his eyes.
We recite our vows and prayers.
I can't help feeling surprise.

How does God turn a sinful life
Into a life of blessing,
Like lifeless mannequins made beautiful
By skillful window dressing?

How was I changed from the person I was
Into the person that I am now?
As we leave the church and you wave good-bye,
It doesn't seem to matter *how*.

Trust in the LORD with all your heart and lean not on your own understanding; in all your ways acknowledge him, and he will make your paths straight.

Proverbs 3:5,6

If you have any encouragement from being united with Christ, if any comfort from his love, if any fellowship with the Spirit, if any tenderness and compassion, then make my joy complete by being like-minded, having the same love, being one in spirit and purpose.

Philippians 2:1,2

Wagons

I was calling a doctor's office to make an appointment. "Your name, please," the receptionist said. "Um, could you spell that?" "Okay, I got your first name. Now could you spell your last name again? Wow! What a name! Is that German?" I was immediately reminded of the day when I first met my husband. I saw his name in print before I heard it pronounced. What a whopper of a name! I had no idea how to say it. When he told me how to pronounce it, he said, "Just think of putting wagons together—wagon connect." My husband has a way of making things easy.

I spelled the name again for the receptionist, answered that it was indeed German, and tried to help by offering her the *connecting-wagons* thing. She didn't seem impressed.

It occurred to me at that moment, however, that my husband's family name reflects the act of making a family. One's family really is like a wagon, connected in some way to many other wagons—our extended family wagons and our church family wagons. Together we are like a real wagon train on a quest, living the lives mapped out for us by God.

As part of God's plan, my husband is at the front of our wagon. He pulls, choosing the direction in which we need to go, keeping his eyes on the path that God has set for him.

I am at the back of the wagon. I push. I support my husband. If I think he might be going a little off course, I tap his shoulder and point to the right path. If he seems to be leading us in the right direction, I pat his back and smile. We nourish each other.

Our children riding in the wagon will have to keep their balance so as not to fall out. We'll each have a hand ready to catch one of them should the need arise. They will watch and learn. Someday they will need to push and pull their own family wagons. The wagon shifts and jostles as new children arrive. But there will always be enough room, even if it sometimes feels a bit cramped.

There are times when the wagon must climb in order to get us where we are going. Emotional hills, financial hills, hills of illness or grief—they make us all struggle. But we struggle together as a unit. The heavy load can become a burden. But, even when my husband looks tired and pale, he must keep going, and he does.

I pray for him. I push as hard as I can. I pray for myself. The Holy Spirit gives us the energy to keep going—the spiritual energy.

The children also help by keeping the load as light as possible. They sense the struggle and throw extra baggage over the side. We will, by God's grace, always make it over the hill. When we do, we all heave a collective sigh of relief and triumph.

Just as difficult as going uphill is the difficulty of going down a particularly large hill. The wagon moves so fast we can scarcely keep up. Occasionally the wagon flings out of control. Dad gets caught up in the excitement and forgets his job.

At first going downhill seems easy; I don't have to push. I can think about other things. I can do things that are just for me. Then, suddenly, I find I am being left behind. The wagon is moving too fast, and I can't keep up. I can no longer reach my husband's shoulder and have to call loudly after him instead. The little ones become frightened. They hold on tightly with white knuckles and cry with fear in their eyes. What began as an exciting ride quickly turns into one fraught with danger and stress. We all hope that we will get control again soon.

Jesus always brings us back, assures us that we are forgiven, and tells us to get back on his path.

All the ups and downs are worth the effort when the smooth ride comes. It is at this time that Dad can pull the wagon with just a finger and point out pretty and interesting things as we travel. He enjoys sharing God's Word and God's love with us. I hardly have to push at all. Now and then I can even jump on the back for a little ride. It's then that I hug my family a little more closely.

The children laugh, learn, and sometimes take rides on Mommy's and Daddy's shoulders along the route. They so want to be part of the pulling and pushing.

Through all of these times, we can see and hear—before, behind, and beside us—the other wagons of our Christian friends and families. We are a wagon train connected to one another and to our Creator-God, our Redeemer-God and his Spirit. The Lord leads, and we follow.

When Satan attacks, we circle the wagons in prayer. If a wagon wheel breaks, others in the train are ready to help. When one wagon gets lost, the others go in search. All the while, our wagon train keeps its eyes on Jesus and the prize of life with him in his eternal promised land.

He stilled the storm to a whisper; the waves of the sea were hushed. They were glad when it grew calm, and he guided them to their desired haven. Let them give thanks to the LORD for his unfailing love and his wonderful deeds for men.

Psalm 107:29-31

A longing fulfilled is sweet to the soul. . . .

Proverbs 13:19

Brown Cake
and Lightning

They say every wedding has its problems. I've even heard it said that a wedding without any problems means a marriage that is full of them. I knew that our wedding wouldn't be like those happily-ever-after storybook weddings, and I didn't much care. With only weeks to plan and an extremely busy (and not wealthy) bride and groom, this wedding didn't have a chance of matching the fairy-tale version.

So, when our photographer failed to show up, I didn't worry; we'd have snapshots. When my self-done hairstyle fell apart and left one big funny-looking curl in the middle of my forehead, I consoled myself with the thought that I was beautiful to the groom anyway. When I forgot my vows and began to giggle nervously, well, the pastor pulled me through. In spite of it all, we were married, and we were happy.

Then came the reception. It was an evening wedding in August. We couldn't afford much. We had planned for cake, punch, and fruit, and prayed that everyone would eat dinner before they came.

I started to fall apart when the first bolt of lightning filled the night sky with light and the roar of thunder vibrated the church walls. When I entered the fellowship hall where the guests had already gathered, the first thing I noticed was that the wedding cake, which was supposed to be ivory, had turned out brown. The fruit platters were empty. We were already running out of punch. I hoped the affair would be over soon and we could get on with the honeymoon, but the storm continued. The church hall looked like a steam room, but the people who had gathered there had forgotten to disrobe and were now dripping perspiration onto their wedding finery. Women were taking off their high heels; men were loosening their ties. All were making frequent dashes to the punch bowl.

I closed my eyes, trying to blot the scene from my memory. But in my blindness, my hearing became acute. Go figure. Of all the voices in the room, chatting about this and that, I heard my mother's most clearly saying to my brother: "Quick, run to the store and buy some punch fixings. We're out, and nobody's leaving!"

I went to a window and watched lightning shoot across the sky as my brother ran to his car. I wished I was running through the rain with him. I searched for someplace to hide. I wanted to be invisible.

My husband saw me standing there and came over to join me. "Isn't the storm beautiful?" he asked. "Look at that lightning! And this cake is delicious. Want some?"

"It's brown!" I said.

"Oh. Yep, I guess it is brown, but it's good. Look at that lightning!"

I glared at him. This was a disaster in the making. It didn't work. Then, suddenly, everything seemed okay.

Anyone who had come to see how nice my hair looked or how pretty the cake was or how good the food would be hadn't come for the right reasons. God had brought us together and allowed us to share our union with friends and family members who cared. (Even older brothers who cared enough to go buy more punch.) Our marriage would not be perfect, just as our wedding had not been perfect. But God was still in control—just as he had controlled the lightning and thunder and, yes, even the brown cake. The cake was, after all, delicious; just as our lives together on earth and our eternity with Jesus in heaven would be. I took a bite of cake and marveled at the power and wisdom of a God who is always in control.

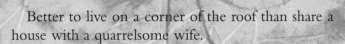

Better to live on a corner of the roof than share a house with a quarrelsome wife.

Proverbs 25:24

Better a dry crust with peace and quiet than a house full of feasting, with strife.

Proverbs 17:1

Hammering Crabs

On our second night as husband and wife, we were already using hammers—on crabs. We pounded until their tough shells splintered. We carefully pulled out the sweet meat; dipped it into messy, drippy melted butter; savored every bite; and then threw the garbage into plastic buckets on the floor by our table. There's nothing better on a honeymoon than an all-you-can-eat blue crab dinner at a beachside restaurant in Florida.

It certainly wasn't the kind of meal you could enjoy together on a first date—butter dripping down your chin, bits of shell under your fingernails, that lovely fishy smell. And just how much crab can one person eat, anyway?

For a honeymoon, though, it was perfect—one of the best of my memories. I remember most of all the loud cracking as the hammers hit the hard shells, competing with the country music on the jukebox. How much my husband looked like a kid in that little plastic bib! And how many buckets we filled with empty shells! We spent hours at that place, filling our bellies and enjoying each other's company.

Part of the reason it was so perfect was that crab is my favorite food, but it also reminded me of marriage itself. Marriage, like crabmeat, is one of the sweetest treats in life with which God blesses us. But sometimes it requires a lot of hard work to get to the good stuff. Our hard, crusty, sinful shells have to be pounded away in order to find the sweetness of our changed person within. That's what distinguishes a Christian marriage from others. Jesus is there working in our hearts, while we're savoring the best that life in him has to offer.

It takes time to get to know each other, to find contentment in a marriage. You have to be ready to throw away the garbage and leave it in the bucket on the floor. Our times of prayer and Bible study together are like butter on the crab. In the end the marriage might be messy, but that's what bibs are for.

I thank my God every time I remember you.

Philippians 1:3

You are a garden fountain, a well of flowing water streaming down from Lebanon.

Song of Songs 4:15

Mosquitoes, Hemingway, and the Red Rooster Inn

"Camping? In a tent? On your honeymoon? I don't think so. Here's some money. Please stay in a motel."

I hate admitting that my brother was right, but he was. We arrived in the Florida Keys, found a beautiful camping spot in a state park, made plans to go snorkeling, and pitched our tent. We were so excited—until the mosquitoes arrived—all ten million of them. I grew up in Florida. I knew about mosquitoes. But this was ridiculous. They were everywhere. They were big and nasty. Within minutes we were swatting and itching all over. I was prepared, though. I had brought along insect repellent. What I wasn't prepared for was just how unromantic the smell and feel of bug repellent really was.

The last straw was a thunderstorm that arrived about dawn. Later that day, with the soggy tent hastily packed away, we checked into the Red Rooster Inn. When the rain stopped, we went snorkeling. Then we decided to tour the Hemingway House.

I had been to the Hemingway House a number of times before. I had been there alone; I had been there with other friends. I thought I had seen it all. To my surprise I found myself seeing and appreciating things I had never noticed before. My husband and I talked about the many cats, the furniture, Hemingway's books, the swimming pool. We talked about what kind of person Ernest Hemingway must have been.

Something about being together with my husband opened my eyes to view places in a new and exciting way. With what other person in the world could I have so appreciated the old attic room of the Red Rooster Inn as reruns of *The Waltons* played on television? Who else could have made my mind so free?

It's just another of the amazing things about our God's generosity. He gives us such a huge capacity for feeling and for thought. Then he gives us those few very special people who are able to bring out our potential, who open us to new possibilities of understanding and insight, and through this sharing they bring us much joy. Those few people can make even mosquitoes and rain-soaked tents a happy adventure.

I have learned the secret of being content in any and every situation, whether well fed or hungry, whether living in plenty or in want. I can do everything through him who gives me strength.

Philippians 4:12,13

Do not store up for yourselves treasures on earth, where moth and rust destroy, and where thieves break in and steal. But store up for yourselves treasures in heaven, where moth and rust do not destroy, and where thieves do not break in and steal. For where your treasure is, there your heart will be also.

Matthew 6:19-21

We Do Things Differently Here

So, I'm tooling around the Milwaukee, Wisconsin area in my little car, checking out the scenery, staying in the right lane so faster cars can go by. I'm liking the place fairly well for an outsider and enjoying the pretty fall leaves. There's a nice tree. Whoa! Where did that car come from? I slam on the brakes quickly. Is there a stalled car in the right lane? No. The car is parked, as are numerous other cars in front of it. No warning sign, no little parallel parking lines, no meters—just cars parked slam bang in front of where I was driving. I put on my left turn signal and wait for a chance to change lanes, while all the native Wisconsinites giggle and point at my Florida license plate.

That was the first of many strange experiences convincing me that "they do things differently *up* in Wisconsin." They even talk a different language. There are the drinking fountains, which they called *bubblers*. And what a surprise to find that people actually drive in snow! I discovered I had to buy an overcoat, gloves, boots, and woolen hats—stuff that had never been part of my wardrobe before. I learned to stop on the street and shovel the snow out of the driveway before heading into the garage after work. I learned the finer points of scraping ice off the windshield. I learned how to make snow angels and build snowmen. I went to fish fries on Friday nights and learned how to eat bratwurst with sauerkraut.

Even after the snow angels, though, I still felt out of place. I missed my home in Florida. I missed the beach. One night I suggested to my husband that we have a cookout—Florida style. We dug a path in the snow from the house to the shed, dragged out the grill, invited some friends, and put on the brats. (Well, okay, the brats part wasn't Florida style, but I was starting to like brats.) I dressed in a bathing suit (and an overcoat) and put on beach music. My husband did a marvelous job of playing along, even calling the snowman a sand sculpture. His friends thought we were a bit strange. But, in the end, I felt happy about who I was, where I had come from, where I was at the moment, and where my husband and I would be in the future.

That was when I started saying, "Home is where the husband is." But, truth be told, home can be anywhere, because God is everywhere. It doesn't matter if you're living in chest-high snowdrifts or beach sand, green grass or brown hills, mountains or valleys.

On the other hand, if we never quite feel at home here on earth, it's because our hearts are already residing in heaven. Because heaven is our real home, we can be truly content, no matter how differently things are done *way up* or *way down* here.

There is a time for everything, and a season for every activity under heaven:

a time to be born and a time to die,
a time to plant and a time to uproot,
a time to kill and a time to heal,
a time to tear down and a time to build,
a time to weep and a time to laugh,
a time to mourn and a time to dance,
a time to scatter stones and a time to gather them,
a time to embrace and a time to refrain,
a time to search and a time to give up,
a time to keep and a time to throw away,
a time to tear and a time to mend,
a time to be silent and a time to speak,
a time to love and a time to hate,
a time for war and a time for peace.

Ecclesiastes 3:1-8

Let them praise his name with dancing and make music to him with tambourine and harp.

Psalm 149:3

Grandpa

It was Saturday. My husband was working at his office, putting in extra hours on top of the usual overtime. I was sitting cross-legged on the floor in front of the television watching a PBS special on swing music—crying. I was six weeks pregnant with my first child and overwhelmed by the emotion of it. The feelings I had about this baby seemed so immense I decided I had to share them with him or her. So, I began to write my thoughts and feelings down.

I told the baby how sick I felt and how we were both living on Goldfish crackers. I told the baby what Daddy was up to at that moment and how lonely I felt. I told the baby I hoped he or she liked big band music as much as I did. That's when Grandpa crossed my mind, not my grandpa but the baby's. I said out loud, "This was your Granddaddy's favorite music." That's when I realized *why* I was crying. It wasn't just hormones or the joy of expecting a child. It was the music.

My mom and dad loved to dance together. When my parents danced, they were exquisite. They flowed across the floor—hands together, hands apart—always a fluid unit. In fact, most everyone liked to dance with my dad, especially me. I would like to say my dad taught me how to jitterbug, but the truth is he just knew how to lead. I didn't have to do anything but let the music take me and let his hands guide me the way he wanted me to go. I felt safe and happy. It was like flying.

"In the Mood" was one of the songs my parents liked to dance to the most. Whenever I hear it, I get teary-eyed. I miss my dad, and the thing I miss most is the dancing.

Someone started singing "I Get a Kick Out of You" on the PBS documentary. I wrote to my baby, "I can't wait to feel you kick."

I wish my dad could have met his grandchild. He adored babies. I felt a pang of regret. I knew my parents had been disappointed with my young adulthood. I didn't date the right kinds of men. I didn't cling to the high moral standards they set for me. But they loved me anyway. My dad would have been happy to know that I married a man of integrity, a man of faith, a good father like himself. I told the baby that we would all be together in heaven someday, and I held back my tears with a smile. I remembered the music and the dance. I remembered the joy of being led by my father with beauty and grace.

Our heavenly Father leads us with beauty and grace as in a dance of two kindred spirits who know each other's moves quite intimately. Sometimes we rebel, as I did. We miss his divine signals and spin away from our instructor. Praise God that he sent Jesus to draw us back to his lead! The security of dancing through life in the hands of God can give us the heady feeling that we are flying. Praise God that someday my father will know that I turned out okay. And someday, in heaven, my baby will meet my dad, and they will hum together some old swing songs. Then we will all dance the dances of praise.

As a mother comforts her child, so will I comfort you.

Isaiah 66:13

The eternal God is your refuge, and underneath are the everlasting arms.

Deuteronomy 33:27

The Day We Bought the Rocking Chair

I was pregnant and fat and not at all in a good mood. Still, I was feeling hopeful. This day seemed to be one of promise. My husband, my partner in this whole pregnancy thing, was going shopping with me.

First we bought a new vacuum cleaner. I was getting too big to vacuum comfortably. When you're expecting the first baby, you can use it as an excuse. Of course, as with all men, my husband had to have the right tool for the job. I waited in the appliance store aisle, all fat and moody, as he chose the machine he wanted—one that we could afford. Then we, me still fat and him getting moodier, went looking for a rocking chair.

We looked in secondhand stores, new furniture stores, and bargain stores. We looked at rocker after rocker, but nothing suited me.

"This one is cheap," he'd say.

"It creaks and it's falling apart. That one is beautiful."

"Yep, and if we were rich you could have it."

Finally, at a discount furniture store after hours of searching, I sat in a gliding chair. It didn't rock; it just moved smoothly back and forth. My feet were aching. I was ready to go home. But as I sat in that chair, I immediately felt calm and comfortable, like I could sit in that chair through endless nights of teething and tummy aches. I could be a mommy in that chair.

"Don't even look at the price; I don't want to know. Just strap me and the chair on top of the car. I'm not moving."

My ever-practical husband said, "Get up, you're sitting on the price tag."

I stood up and closed my eyes.

"Hmm. Not too bad," he said. "We'll take it."

It came in a box, in pieces, and when we arrived at home the first order of business, even before trying out the new vacuum cleaner, was to put the chair together. I lay on my back on the floor, alternately watching my husband work and staring at the ceiling. He looked like a dad. And more than the nursery, the crib, or the blankets so lovingly made by our friends—that chair represented security. As I watched it being put together, I realized what a wonderful support system I had. My husband would always be there putting things together. Friends and family would always be there when times got hard. Most of all, my loving God, who had made this new life within me possible, would now support me, comfort me, and glide me through parenthood as only the all-powerful and all-loving God could do. His love would be my rocking chair, where I could be soothed and cuddled, warm and safe. When I finally sat in my chair after the long day, I was still fat; but now I was fat and happy.

Clap your hands, all you nations; shout to God with cries of joy.

Psalm 47:1

Worship the LORD with gladness; come before him with joyful songs.

Psalm 100:2

He Clapped

He was seven months old—loud, grumpy, and cute. He wasn't
even thinking about crawling, and he couldn't bear to be lying
down. He always wanted to be held, or on rare occasions he
wanted to sit up and play with his toys. Every time a toy got out
of his reach, he screamed and cried for Mom to get it. It was really
starting to bug me. Why didn't he crawl, or scoot, or even try to
move? Why was he such a grump?

Then it happened. He was sitting on the floor, watching me
iron his father's shirts. I had the radio turned up loud, and I was
singing. I looked at him; he looked at me. Then he put his
hands together, and they made a sound! I cheered; he smiled.
He kept clapping his hands together as the music played. Suddenly, I didn't care if he could crawl!

My son has always been surrounded by music. We've been
singing to him since before he was born. He listened as we
played pat-a-cake with him in a sing-song rhythm. In fact, he
was already a welcomed member of the church choir.

Our son had learned the joy of music. I had learned the joy
of him. We both knew the joy of Jesus, even though my son
did not yet fully understand that joy. I continued to teach him
about music and about his Savior; that was, and still is, my job.
I know that he will make joyful noise unto the Lord forever.

No temptation has seized you except what is common to man. And God is faithful; he will not let you be tempted beyond what you can bear. But when you are tempted, he will also provide a way out so that you can stand up under it.

1 Corinthians 10:13

Strengthen the feeble hands, steady the knees that give way.

Isaiah 35:3

Handprints

In ten minutes the doorbell would ring and a whole slew of people would be "dropping by" to take a look at our new house—every nook and cranny. And I couldn't find my husband! He was supposed to be cleaning. Instead, after I ran upstairs about to pull my hair out, I found him sitting on the edge of the bed, Windex and a rag in hand, staring at the mirrored closet door.

"What are you doing?" I bellowed. "You are supposed to be cleaning the glass. Why are you just sitting there?"

He patted the bed beside him. I sat down anxiously. He pointed at a spot on the mirror and smiled. There it was—a tiny little handprint belonging to our son. He was just learning to stand, and when there was nothing solid that he could pull himself up on, he begged to be propped up—anywhere. I understood even as my husband pointed. I was so proud of that handprint—filled with the earnest motherly desire to keep my boy just the way he appeared in my mind that very moment.

"Maybe we could leave it," I said. "No one would notice."

My husband, who perhaps had been loafing after all, said, "He'll make more, honey." Then he squirted Windex, wiped, and the handprint was gone.

Later I pondered just how special that handprint was to me. I thought about the wonder of a mother's love for her children.

We are God's own dear children. Jesus died in order to restore us to that precious relationship. I wonder if there are handprints etched in God's mind, times during our spiritual growing-up that were special. Is there a handprint each time one of us stands by the Spirit's power, shaken but unyielding, against temptation? Is there a print every time one of us returns to God's enduring Word to find our way and our strength? Does God treasure the greasy, messy little handprints we leave when we lean on him, realizing we cannot stand alone?

I thank God for giving me someone to teach, someone to treasure as God treasures us. I thank God that he loves me, that he accepts the gifts I give to him with my dirty human hands—hands that he has made clean.

The LORD watches over you—the LORD is your shade at your right hand; the sun will not harm you by day, nor the moon by night.

Psalm 121:5,6

Every good and perfect gift is from above, coming down from the Father of the heavenly lights, who does not change like shifting shadows.

James 1:17

A Moonlight View

Next to me in bed lies a little boy who's having trouble getting to sleep.

"Please, Mommy, can I stay with you and Daddy, just for a little while?"

A bit annoyed but too tired to say no, I've agreed to let him crawl in.

It's too dark to see his face, but the bright moon shines through the lace curtain onto a tiny infant hand that is clutching the tassel of a blanket, squeezing it, and rubbing it in a slow, gentle rhythm that is as lovely as any lullaby.

The little fingers slow to a stop, and I can hear his breathing get deeper and more peaceful. At last, he has found sleep, and I too can close my eyes.

I discover, however, that I cannot so easily close my own eyes on that tiny hand illuminated by the soft light of the moon. The soft light has made things appear the way they should. At other times, in other circumstances, those same beautiful, little hands can seem so trying in the harsh light of day, but not so in the light of God's perfect pale moonlight. Under that light everything in my view seems veiled in peace.

My child, myself, and my family were all made perfect in spite of our weaknesses. Our souls are no longer exposed to the broad, harsh light of divine judgment but are, instead, illuminated in the gentle, forgiving light of Christ's love. We can now rest quietly nestled next to our Father-God and reflect his light as beautifully as any lullaby.

Remember this: Whoever turns a sinner from the error of his way will save him from death and cover over a multitude of sins.

James 5:20

Praise be to the God and Father of our Lord Jesus Christ, the Father of compassion and the God of all comfort, who comforts us in all our troubles, so that we can comfort those in any trouble with the comfort we ourselves have received from God.

2 Corinthians 1:3,4

The Quilt

The congregation was fairly small and full of older retirees. There were very few young families. We felt at home, though. The older folks adopted us as their own and made our children their grandchildren and loved us as they loved their own families. They made us happy.

One Sunday after church just before our second child was born, I stood holding an exquisite quilt given to me by a wonderful lady who had become like a mother to me. This woman always made a quilt and a knitted blanket for each new baby born into the congregation. I, who cannot sew a lick, marveled at the beauty of this thing. I asked her some questions about her quilting.

"I love the children," she said. "The quilts are my own way of giving each child some special thing to cherish. Often the blankets I make become their favorites. That makes me feel good. Blankets can be so special—not only useful to keep warm but also for comfort and companionship."

Then she showed me a little flaw in the quilt and explained that it wasn't perfect. She said this with a little smile of apology. But somehow that flaw made the quilt even more special to me. It reminded me that this beautiful piece of handiwork had been made by her loving and caring hands—hands that belonged to someone who would always remember and love my baby almost as much as I would, almost as much as Jesus *does*.

As I stood holding the quilt, I couldn't help but think how our Christian lives are like that marvelous quilt. In communities all over the world we work on little squares of the blanket of God's love. We stitch in the smile of a friend here, the arms of a neighbor there, and the eyes of a new baby in another place. We share the good news, and through our efforts God makes a fantastic pattern—a picture, if you will—of his people whom he loves.

This life of a Christian is a team effort. Those who have extra material and thread send it along to those who have less. We work hard and then ask God to accomplish his plans through our efforts.

In the end God's quilts always turn out the same. He blesses our work and our prayers, and the blanket grows into a work of unsurpassed craftsmanship and beauty.

Now and then one of us misses a stitch. The Lord takes those missed stitches and turns them into something quite exquisite—and useful. The blanket of his love is completed with people like ourselves. We will, in turn, always be there to keep one another warm, to comfort each other when we are lonely or frightened, and to be favorite companions in good times and in bad.

Put your finger here; see my hands. Reach out your hand and put it into my side. Stop doubting and believe.

John 20:27

Because you have seen me, you have believed; blessed are those who have not seen and yet have believed.

John 20:29

Touch and See

She touches my face, rubs it, squeezes it. If I'm not holding her, it's Daddy's face or that of a close friend or relative. Her brother's face will do in a pinch if he sits next to her on the floor. If she gets hurt, she sucks her thumb, reaches out, and is soothed. After the hurt goes away, her eyes close in sleep, or after a short time, she goes on to play. The voices that speak to her, the eyes that watch over her—they are her anchor. But it won't do just to hear them and see them; she must touch them in order to know what they mean to her. Through the touch she knows what it means to be loved and protected.

Seeing her I am reminded of the disciple Thomas. It wasn't enough for him to be *told* that Jesus was alive. It wasn't even enough for him to *see* Jesus alive. To a skeptic like Thomas, there is always a chance that it might be a lie or a trick. But when Thomas *touched* the nail prints in the Savior's hands and *felt* the place where the spear had pierced his Lord's side, he had all the proof he needed to know that Jesus was alive.

We all need that kind of reassurance every now and then—in Communion we receive Christ himself, his body and blood, and through this we experience his physical touch. It strengthens us and fills our hearts with renewed faith that tells us all is well; God is with us, loving us, protecting us, and caring for our every need.

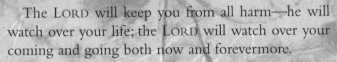

The LORD will keep you from all harm—he will watch over your life; the LORD will watch over your coming and going both now and forevermore.

Psalm 121:7,8

Commit to the LORD whatever you do, and your plans will succeed. In his heart a man plans his course, but the LORD determines his steps.

Proverbs 16:3,9

God's Sense
of Humor

I watched the television commercial and laughed out loud. A little boy about a year old was sitting quietly in his playpen, watching his daddy work, enjoying the sights and sounds of the computer, printer, fax, and such. An idyllic picture. Telecommunicating.

Not in my house! I sit down at the computer to write an e-mail or play a game and in they come, banging on the keyboard, grabbing the mouse, fighting over toys, asking the millionth mommy question of the day. The funny thing is that I once naively thought children were like the passive kid in that TV commercial. Now I know I was wrong. Such children exist only in a fairy-tale world.

It's true that kids know a lot today. When I was a kid, a mouse had four legs and fur. My kids know a lot more about that plastic thing that goes click, click, click than they do about any rodent. And that little bit of knowledge is, well, not dangerous, but incredibly annoying.

Some friends of ours have a little girl the same age as our son. She actually plays with toys by herself, and she doesn't ask a million questions throughout the day. To me she hardly seems real. Her mom talks seriously about working out of their home. Again I laugh out loud! Okay, so it *is* just *my* kids; or maybe it's their not-so-disciplined mom.

My mother says it's the curse. You know what I mean—I was a rotten kid, so my mom cursed me to have rotten kids. Some of our friends are a bit kinder. They simply call it "God's sense of humor."

I continue to wonder why I have wild children. It must be for the same reasons I can't seem to do any adult things in my home.

Sometimes I wish I could lock my children in their rooms and pretend I didn't have them. Instead, I keep telling myself that the Lord knows what's good for me and that my children are truly blessings.

I have a tendency to want certain things—lots of things— according to my timetable and my way. I call these tendencies my *crocodile pits*. I have a habit of jumping into my crocodile pits with both feet, never really giving much thought to whether God wants me to be there or not, and certainly not expecting to get bitten. The miracle is that even when I don't wait for the Lord, even when I take things into my own hands, somehow I don't get eaten alive. God pulls me out of the pit— even when it's a crocodile pit of my own making. The process of my own maturation seems to be making me appreciate just how active God is in my daily life. On the other hand, I guess I've always been aware that my life has required the attentions of quite a few more angels than most.

I've learned, however, that my children tend to keep me out of the crocodile pits. It may be that God has needed to reassign a few angels to other duty. In any case, his strategy has been remarkably effective. The insatiable curiosity of my kids keeps me on my toes. Their amazing creativity feeds my own creativity in the service of God. I'm so busy answering that million and first question-of-the-day that I haven't got the time to look at a pit, much less jump into it. The crocodiles are probably still ferociously hungry, and some of God's angels are still watching over me lest I slip in, but with my kids I've been given the kinds of challenges that will keep me from the pit's edge.

I guess I am where I need to be. Maybe, when my children get a little older and I become a bit more mature (whenever that may be), my son can teach me how to telecommunicate.

Do not be anxious about anything, but in everything, by prayer and petition, with thanksgiving, present your requests to God.

Philippians 4:6

We do not know what we ought to pray for, but the Spirit himself intercedes for us with groans that words cannot express.

Romans 8:26

The Haircut

Our family is frugal. (And I do mean frugal!) We made the decision when we had our first child that I would stay home to care for him and we would live on my husband's salary. We are blessed with having a nice place to live—the comforts of a modest American home. What I personally am *not* blessed with is the ability to cut hair. I can cut hair, mind you; it just doesn't exactly look like the latest fashionable style. So, when my frugal (and I do mean frugal) husband came home one day with a set of clippers and a haircutting video, I sighed a heavy sigh and said, "Do I have to?" I said this with exactly the same whine our children sometimes use. Just like that: *Do I have to?*

My husband, treating me just like one of the children, said, "Yes, you do."

These days my husband's hair has become quite the topic of conversation around town. People, whether intending to be nice or to make a joke, tell him they like his new haircut. Of course he totally misses the irony in their voices and is most gracious in his response: "Thanks, my wife did it."

Ooohhh, please tell me he didn't say that. How embarrassing!

Tonight is another one of those nights. He has come home and asked our son to take care of his little sister while Mommy cuts Daddy's hair. Groan! So I say a little prayer: "Lord, make it come out decent this time. I know this isn't one of my talents, but could you maybe send a haircutting angel or something? I don't want to give him that butchered look again."

Okay, I remember hearing somewhere that we are supposed to take everything to God in prayer. Maybe this prayer isn't as dumb as it sounds. Now, I wonder what God's answer will be: "Yes, I want my servant to look good as he goes about his daily business," or "No, I want a good laugh."

People say, "Beauty is in the eye of the beholder," so I shut up and started to cut. The verdict isn't in yet at the time of this writing. But I learned a valuable lesson: there are just some times in life in which we have little choice in the matter; we just do what we have to and move on, letting God decide how everyone else will react.

Your word is a lamp to my feet and a light for my path.

Psalm 119:105

How beautiful on the mountains are the feet of those who bring good news, who proclaim peace, who bring good tidings, who proclaim salvation. . . .

Isaiah 52:7

Sand in My Shoes

Before I had children I hardly ever got sand in my shoes. Now it's almost a daily occurrence. It gets in my shoes when I step into the garden to keep my kids from picking the green tomatoes. It accumulates whenever I push them on the swing, catch them as they go down the slide, or stand watch as they cross the monkey bars at the park. That little bit of sand can be easily dumped out.

On other occasions, it is a different story. Once the children decided that my shoes made good sandcastle molds for their sandbox. They tried to get all the sand out when they were finished building the sandcastle, but, when I put my clean stockinged foot into the shoe, I felt the squishy leftovers. Thinking that what I was feeling was a smooshed frog, I jumped back out of my shoes, shivering in disgust.

Since then, however, it has occurred to me that our shoes get the dirtiest—inside and out—when we are the busiest. I mean, when we're working the hardest or having the most fun, who cares about a little sand? It takes trudging through a lot of sand and mud to share the gospel with other people. It takes hard work to be a disciple, as all of us are.

The Bible tells us that our feet are beautiful when we bring the good news to someone. So, my muddy shoes that have worked in the garden and my mother-shoes that were filled with sandbox sand remind me that I can't be doing God's work if my feet are always perfectly clean.

"Not by might nor by power, but by my Spirit,"
says the LORD Almighty.

Zechariah 4:6

So is my word that goes out from my mouth: It
will not return to me empty, but will accomplish
what I desire and achieve the purpose for which I
sent it.

Isaiah 55:11

More Than We Expect

I had a bad attitude the whole week of vacation Bible school. We'd been away most of the summer—conventions, vacations, travel. VBS hadn't been planned. I was tired; my husband was tired; and the few people who had volunteered were asking for guidance. There were craft projects to get ready. The program hadn't been advertised enough, so I didn't expect many children. To put it bluntly, I was not serving the Lord joyfully.

As it turned out, I did have a class to teach—three rowdy boys who didn't seem interested in learning much about Jesus. My one-year-old crawled under the table, played peek-a-boo, and disrupted lessons. The boys played with her, ignored me, and made smart-alecky comments about everything. Crafts that should have taken two days to complete were finished in ten minutes, and all the children clamored to go outside and play. It wasn't the best of weeks, but we survived.

Then one of the boys from my class showed up at Sunday school. He hadn't been there in months. I was surprised. He hugged me. I was even more surprised. He said: "Teacher, I remember one of the Bible verses we had to memorize at vacation Bible school. Do you want to hear it?" He said the entire verse perfectly and beamed a huge smile in my direction. I told him it was a wonderful verse to remember and reminded him that the verse he had memorized would help him in many situations. He listened to me for a change.

In fact, the response from that year's vacation Bible school was better than anyone had expected it to be. I had hoped for a good turnout and a smooth week. I had prayed that I would get through it without losing my mind. God had a little more in mind. He didn't just want me to get through it; he wanted me to know the joy involved in doing the work, disorganized as it seemed. This time, he allowed me to see some actual results from the teaching of his Word. There hadn't been a hundred children at vacation Bible school willingly listening and happily learning. There hadn't been a feeling of accomplishment at a job well done. There had been at least one boy who, by God's grace and the working power of his Spirit, remembered something vital. That was a rare and wonderful gift.

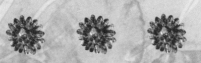

When I want to do good, evil is right there with me. For in my inner being I delight in God's law; but I see another law at work in the members of my body, waging war against the law of my mind and making me a prisoner of the law of sin at work within my members. What a wretched man I am! Who will rescue me from this body of death? Thanks be to God—through Jesus Christ our Lord!

Romans 7:21-25

Here is a trustworthy saying that deserves full acceptance: Christ Jesus came into the world to save sinners—of whom I am the worst. But for that very reason I was shown mercy so that in me, the worst of sinners, Christ Jesus might display his unlimited patience as an example for those who would believe on him and receive eternal life.

1 Timothy 1:15,16

The Mommy Monster

As I sit in front of the computer and lose at solitaire for the umpteenth time, I start to question my purpose. It is 2:30 A.M., and my one-year-old is laughing. Normally laughter is something I appreciate in a baby, but not at 2:30 A.M. It is at times like these that I turn into the Mommy Monster. I feel terrible about this transformation, but I'm too tired and too frustrated to be a normal human being. (Or maybe a normal human being already *is* a monster.) Maybe I'm just too tired to be what God wants me to be.

Just today I screamed at my son, put him in his room, and slammed the door. I didn't finish the laundry, didn't cook the most tasty meal ever concocted, and complained about something my husband was doing when he was just trying to help. The real truth is that I'm not only a Mommy Monster but also a wife monster and homemaker monster. If I still had a career, I most likely would be a work monster too.

"We're losing again," I tell my child. Again come the giggles. She doesn't seem to grasp what it is that we're losing, or that I'm about to morph into a monster again. She just wants my undivided attention at what I consider to be the wrong time of the day.

Finally, she puts her head on my shoulder as I switch to a different screen on the computer. Not feeling particularly warm and fuzzy toward her at the moment, I try to find something that will soothe my anger. I quietly start to compile a list of everyone who loves my little girl—starting with Jesus, then Daddy, her grandmas, her grandpa, her brother, the rest of our family, and friends. I end the list with the Mommy Monster. She giggles again softly, but this time she is sucking her thumb and her eyes are closed. I know that after more than an hour of rocking, singing, talking, and playing computer games, she is almost asleep. I breathe a sigh of relief and kiss her on the cheek.

We are all monsters. Human beings are born monsters. None of us, on our own, can love the way that God wants us to love. None of us can live the way he wants us to live. We are often quite adept at making messes of our relationships and failing in our responsibilities. I consider myself one of the best mess-makers. In the moments that I realize I am being a monster, I vacillate between excusing this behavior because, after all, I am just human, and condemning myself to being a monster forever—sure that I will never do anything right.

But one thing that will always be right for my daughter is the love list that starts with Jesus. He loves me, and her—and the boss that I once couldn't stand, my husband, my son, and on and on. Jesus loved us enough to pay for all our monstrous behaviors, words, and thoughts. He redeemed this Mommy Monster from her sins and keeps on delivering her from her own self-absorbed messes in the making. This Mommy Monster is all things to him and he is everything to her, as well. He is mother and father, brother and sister, and friend—none of whom ever treat this Mommy Monster the way she deserves to be treated. He understands my frustration and forgives my reactions. He gives me the power to change. I don't have to be a monster any longer. I am free to be the loving person God intended me to be.

"Sleep well," whispers the mommy, who remembers that her love always begins with Jesus. "Tomorrow will be a new day."

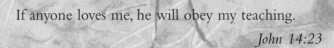

If anyone loves me, he will obey my teaching.

John 14:23

He guards the course of the just and protects the way of his faithful ones.

Proverbs 2:8

Obey First,
Ask Questions Later

I was trying to impress upon my preschooler the importance of listening to and obeying his parents. He had gotten into trouble numerous times during the day because he was ignoring me. He continued to do the things I'd asked him not to do, or he refused to do the things I wanted him to do. I was frustrated to the point of screaming. But this time—by God's grace—I resisted the urge. During one of his many time-outs, I decided to tell him a story about myself as a child—and about my father, the grandfather he never had the privilege of knowing.

My father was far from perfect. He made many parenting mistakes. Yet, I remembered him fondly as my son and I talked.

My father always tried to make my brothers and me understand how much he loved us. He taught us that it was essential that we do as he said. Those were his words: *Do as I say*. It was the only way he felt he could keep us safe. It was his primary lesson for life—listen and obey first, ask questions later. He was right, of course. My father had kept me from being hurt or making a big mistake plenty of times.

I tried to impress upon my son that I loved my father dearly, just as my father had always loved me. It was a dramatic moment for me, but my son stared at me blankly for a few seconds and then changed the subject.

I could tell he wasn't getting it, so I embellished a little. We parents have to do what works, you know. So I casually added, "Okay, how about a little story?"

"Is it bedtime?"

"It's close enough. Here's the story."

"One day some members of our family—my mom, dad, older brother, and me—were walking in the woods. There were tall pine trees all around us. They filled the air with a fresh, clean smell. The ground was covered with pine needles and rocks and little lizards that ran away as I stepped near them. I looked up through the limbs of the trees to see the small patches of blue sky and fat white clouds. I listened to the warbled songs of my favorite birds. They were singing a song that sounded like *Bob White, Bob, Bob White*. I thought it was a funny sound.

"Soon I had gotten ahead of the rest of my family. I couldn't see them, but I could still hear my parents talking to my brother behind me. Suddenly my father yelled my name and told me to stop. I did. At that moment I remembered how important it was to listen. I stopped quickly and turned around to look at him. He told me to stay right where I was and not to move a muscle. Then he moved forward quickly, grabbed me, and held me tight. As he lifted me up in his arms, I looked down. A big, fat rattlesnake slithered away through the thick trees. I hadn't seen the snake, but my father had. If I had not listened to him, I might have stepped right on top of that poisonous snake and been bitten."

My son smiled at the story and then asked to go back outside to play. I'm not sure the story happened in the exact same way that I told it. I only know there were many times when listening to my father and my mother made all the difference in my life.

As I watched my son run and jump out in the backyard, I began to better understand what it means to obey—not just obeying those who have some earthly authority over us, but especially obeying our heavenly Father. When we do his will, when we do what the Bible says we ought to do, it not only shows our love for our Savior, but it also confirms his love for us.

As adults we want to make informed decisions. We want to know all the whys and wherefores before committing ourselves to some course of action. Our sinful natures exert pressure, urging us to do those things that will always serve us best. But we can't always see the snake that is curled up right in our path. We don't hear the sound of the rattles or feel a sense of danger. If it was not for God's love for us, we might plunge ahead and step on the snake.

I know this is true. I know because of the many times I have forgotten this truth. Instead of obeying first, I have too often ignored God's warnings.

I've been bitten too. Thankfully, God also has the anti-venom. He heals the wounds and then gently uses his Word to put us back on the right path.

Right then and there I had to stop. This lesson was as much meant for me as for my child. I asked God to help me obey him and to forgive me for my impatience. I prayed that he would give me the resolve to use his Holy Word in place of my angry words whenever my child needed a warning. This turned out to be a daily prayer. I guess we both needed to learn to obey first and ask questions later.

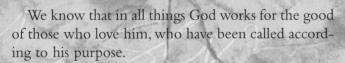

We know that in all things God works for the good of those who love him, who have been called according to his purpose.

Romans 8:28

Charm is deceptive, and beauty is fleeting; but a woman who fears the LORD is to be praised.

Proverbs 31:30

All That He Is

Stirring the soup in the pot,
One child tugging, arms up, pleading with me,
Another crying in the other room.

I stir the soup,
Pat the shoulder,
Answer the cry,
Think about God,
Ask him why
Life is what it is,
And he is who he is.

He is the Creator—
A whole world in six days.
Adam and Eve.
Me.
And the children driving me crazy right now.
Who'll make me happy later.
My ability to make this soup.

He is the provider—
Of every need.
The material comes to mind
As I stir our supper.
His provisions are countless:

The emotional, the mental and, most of all, the spiritual.
Provider of faith,
Giver of the Word,
The Living Word,
The Word and the water,
The bread and the wine—
The real soup of life.

He is the Redeemer—
He paid for me,
Lived for me, died for me, rose for me,
Gave up everything for me . . .
And for this little one tugging at my arm.
He pulled us out of the hot soup,
When we didn't even know we were burning.

He is the Comforter—
The one possible place to turn no matter what the situation,
No matter how distraught or sad or helpless.
Even when I'm not sure
Why making soup makes me sad.

He is my companion—
During the most mundane of moments.
Part of my life as I cook,
Crying with me,
Laughing with me.

He understands my dreams like no one else.
He likes my soup.

He is my purpose—
I was his reason for coming to earth.
He is my reason for being here,
In this kitchen,
In this house,
In this world.
The purpose becomes more evident each day—
Love him,
Make soup.

He is joy—
Joy inexplicable.
All will be right just because he says so.
I know it.
I smile it.
I live it.
Even if there's a time when there is no soup.

He is strength—
To finish the task,
To finish the supper,

To continue the mothering,
To share the nourishment.
I stir the soup.

I am a soup kitchen
For the spiritually homeless.
And he is
All that he is.

I sought the LORD, and he answered me; he delivered me from all my fears.

Psalm 34:4

Let us fix our eyes on Jesus, the author and perfecter of our faith, who for the joy set before him endured the cross, scorning its shame, and sat down at the right hand of the throne of God.

Hebrews 12:2

The Flyby

I was at the computer in my home office, typing. The idea for a story had struck me, and I didn't want to lose it. Both kids were sleeping; there was no time to lose. But after a few short moments, I heard crying from upstairs and ran to retrieve my daughter. *Can't let her wake the older one. If that happens, I'll never get anything done.*

Much to my surprise she seemed willing to play quietly beside me. *I just might be able to get this done.* But then she started running in and out of the room, screaming at me as if some terrible thing were happening. She didn't know the words; she only knew she wanted me. After saying "I'll be there in a minute" several times, I finally got up and followed her into the living room, hoping to see whatever it was and then get right back to work.

The "whatever it was" was a sound in the fireplace. "Yes, honey," I said. "There must be a bird's nest on the roof. Sometimes we can hear them through the fireplace." I went back to work. But the screaming and the tugging at my legs started again, so I went back again.

This time I listened more carefully. Sure enough, the sound was quite loud. Some animal was definitely in the fireplace. I opened the sliding door and listened again. Yep, still there. I knew I needed to stick my head in and look around, but for some unknown reason, fear pushed me away.

About that time my son bounded down the stairs, blanket in hand, and said, "Mommy, what are you doing?"

"There's something in the fireplace."

"A mouse?"

Aha! That's where the fear had come from. A bird I could handle, but I could not deal with a rodent!

"Mom, is it a mouse?"

"I don't know; I'll have to look." I started to stick my head into the fireplace when whatever it was made a sudden movement. I jumped and pulled my head out at the same time—not a smart move. "Ow," I said, rubbing my head.

My son laughed. I glared at him. I tried to look again. No success. Then I started to imagine a rodent scrambling across my toes. "Okay, here's the thing," I confessed. "Mommy's afraid of mice. So if it's a mouse, we will be forced to go and sleep somewhere else until your dad comes home from his trip."

"Don't worry, Mom, Jesus will protect you," came the reassuring reply from my son. Leave it to a child to throw your own words right back in your face.

"Yes, I'm sure he will; but I still can't look."

"Okay, Mom, I'll look."

So my son looked. Then he jumped, bumped his own head, and cried. When I got him calmed down, he told me it looked like a bird. Suddenly I was brave again. I poked my head in and saw the darting eyes, the little beak, and the feathers. Yep, a bird. Ha! And you were so scared. But now it was time to remove the bird. How?

I quickly decided that the bird was not stuck. He had simply fallen down the chimney and was afraid to come out, what with a screeching daughter, crying son, and petrified mother milling about. So I opened the sliding glass door to make a clear path to the outside and told the children we should hide and watch. Of course, at about that time, the family cat decided to come into the room in search of a snack. I snatched her up quickly and took the whole lot of us upstairs to a bedroom.

We hadn't been upstairs more than a minute when my daughter opened the door just a tad, and out the cat went, down the stairs with me in hot pursuit screaming, "Don't eat the bird!"

My screaming made my daughter cry, and my daughter's crying made my son cry. Besides their crying, I frightened the poor cat half to death. She didn't even notice the bird, but bolted through the open door instead and found a place to hide from her frantic owner.

And the bird? Just as I had expected, he had flown from the fireplace the moment we all left him alone. Unfortunately, he had winged his way right past the open door and was trying to escape through the closed kitchen window. The sound of flutter—flutter—thud, flutter—flutter—thud was not pleasant. My little one started to scream again, pointing at the bird and expecting me to do something to rescue it. I searched frantically in the garage for a net or something, knowing there was no bird-catching equipment to be found. I slid the window open, hoping to push out the screen, but it was permanently attached.

Then I saw something I had noticed with frustration many times before. There was a hole in that screen just about the size of the small bird. An overgrown rosebush had pushed through there long ago, and I had been much annoyed with my husband for not replacing the screen. Now I was quite pleased.

I climbed up on the counter next to the sink and stared at the bird—at that long, sharp beak. I wasn't really frightened, but there was what I might term a *palpable tension*. It didn't seem right for human hands to touch this wild animal. He looked at me with the same sort of look, like he wanted more than anything to be away from these unwild things. I slid up near the windowsill beside him and pushed my hand through the hole in the screen. He watched. I removed my hand, and almost instantly he was through the hole, into the air, to the top of a tree, already telling his other little bird friends about his adventure.

My children and I had cups of hot cocoa and talked about the adventure too. Finally, I began to relax. It's rare that anything *that* exciting happens in our home, and I was still shaky.

When the cocoa was gone and we were all calm, it seemed a good time to pray. Having been so close to a creature so magnificently and delicately made, we were led to marvel at the wild beauty of nature and to praise God for his creation. We thanked God for the safe return of the bird to his proper surroundings. We thanked him for his power to keep us calm and to protect us even when we are afraid. We thanked him for one another, with whom we shared the experience. Finally, we thanked God for rescuing us from our entrapment in sin, even as we had rescued the bird from his entrapment in our house. We thanked God for bringing light to our darkness, for providing a way for salvation, and for giving us our saving faith.

I forgot the work I had been doing and spent the evening with those children who had such compassion for God's creature.

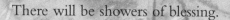

There will be showers of blessing.

Ezekiel 34:26

If you, then, though you are evil, know how to give good gifts to your children, how much more will your Father in heaven give good gifts to those who ask him!

Matthew 7:11

Simple Joys

Every once in a while our Lord provides a nearly perfect morning or afternoon or day, empty of problems and abundant with joys. These seem to me to be little hints of heaven, snapshots of what our lives could have been without sin. I remember one such morning with a fondness that, when brought to mind, actually helps me be more patient on days that aren't so great. The children didn't fight with each other. No one was sent to his or her room. None of them whined or cried for almost four hours. It was magnificent. They asked for music. Mom sought to please.

We popped a Vivaldi tape into the player, and they began to dance. They looked like they were having so much fun, my feet couldn't be still—nor could my arms, legs, torso, or head. I simply had to join in the dance. We danced together; we danced apart; we danced with bears and dollies. We spun around until we were dizzy and jumped in the air pretending to be great ballerinas. One of them left the room and returned with a stool and a spoon to accompany Vivaldi on a makeshift drum. The other found a keyboard with a microphone and played along with the music. They both made up words to go with the sounds.

When the tape ended, they wanted more, but I was too tired to move. So they brought me the volume of the encyclopedia with the section on the human body and asked me to tell them about how God made us. They listened and looked and asked questions. They showed off their little sponge-like minds.

The morning went on in peace and joy until I realized I hadn't started lunch or the laundry yet, and I had to leave them to play alone. Still, they played together, watched television together, and enjoyed each other's company.

When my husband came home for lunch, I wondered if he noticed a difference. I wondered if he knew the blessings—the simple joys we had shared. I wondered if he thought I looked less harried and more friendly than usual. My only regret was that he had not been there to experience these simple miracles. I told myself that there would be many more such days in which he could participate. I smiled, said hello, and proceeded to set the table, all the while thinking of the awesome love God shows us each day.

If anyone speaks, he should do it as one speaking the very words of God. If anyone serves, he should do it with the strength God provides, so that in all things God may be praised through Jesus Christ. To him be the glory and the power for ever and ever. Amen.

1 Peter 4:11

His master replied, "Well done, good and faithful servant! . . . Come and share your master's happiness!"

Matthew 25:23

Something New

Me—standing in the middle of a fabric store,
Holding a bolt of fabric in my arms—
Like holding a baby.

My companion—a wonderful lady
Instructing me to buy four yards—
As if teaching a child.

The sewing machine—sitting on the table,
Waiting for me to touch it—
Like a foundling.

Me again—looking at that machine,
Wondering if I'll figure it out without going crazy—
Like a child studying algebra.

God—reassuring me,
Giving someone to help me—
Like a Father.

Me again—ripping out seams,
Full of excitement for what the future will bring—
Like a child of God receiving his gifts.

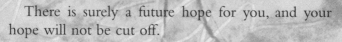

There is surely a future hope for you, and your hope will not be cut off.

Proverbs 23:18

My times are in your hands.

Psalm 31:15

Growing Up

I knew the time was drawing near for the annual women's retreat in northern California. But we had just moved to southern California—I wouldn't be going to the retreat this year. I expected to be melancholy. I expected to miss the other women, the fellowship, the Bible study, the time in the beautiful mountains to relax and reflect. I dared to hope that an airplane ticket would suddenly drop in my lap and my husband would offer to keep the kids.

It never happened. Instead, I began to remember past retreats with hallowed fondness—all the wisdom imparted by women with more experience, all the truths learned from God's Word, the shared tears and laughter, the good food, the hot tub! I remembered boat rides, scenic hikes, and rediscovering the awesomeness of God's creation. Those were times of growing up, the beginnings of learning to be the wife and mother God intended me to be.

I had been apprehensive about moving and reluctant to leave important people behind. It wasn't until I thought back on those retreats that I realized how God had used those times to ready me for my present life.

I the LORD do not change.

Malachi 3:6

For riches do not endure forever, and a crown is not secure for all generations.

Proverbs 27:24

Redistributed

There are times in life when mirrors seem ubiquitous, ominous, terrifying—when just taking a peek brings moans of despair at the loathsome shape of things. The week before my brother-in-law's wedding was one of these times.

Three members of my family were scheduled to be in the wedding party. They had wedding clothes to wear. My husband would shore up his brother, readying the young groom for the task of dealing with one of *us* on a continual basis. He was handsome in his new black suit, as was my son; he would bear the symbolic rings. Our daughter would serve as the flower girl.

Then there was me. While they were ready with their wedding finery, I had been reduced to tears by a simple pane of reflective glass, lamenting the fact that the perfectly gorgeous dress I had planned to wear now revealed all the bulges I had hoped to hide.

I left my two handsome men at home with our young daughter prancing around the house saying, "I going to be a butifoo fower griew and dance at da wedding in my bwide dwess." My mission: one dress and a smidgen of self-confidence.

At the mall I tried on dress after dress. Each time the mirrors called out to me, "You don't look 20 anymore, ha, ha, ha!"

Then I spied a cute little store with cute little items inside. I picked out some dresses in popular polyester prints and headed toward a fitting room. "Whatcha lookin' for?" a teenaged sales clerk asked, stepping out from behind the counter.

"A dress for a wedding," I replied.

"Oh, that yellow one would be great," she said.

It was a nice dress—yellow with blue flowers, almost ankle length, princess waistline. I looked at the dress; I looked at the girl. She was obviously wearing clothing from the store—gray polyester pants with wide bottoms over clunky black shoes and a black tank top with embroidered flowers. Cute. *Very* cute.

Her zeal was infectious, as was her smile. With a new sense of hope, I slipped into the dress and looked confidently into the mirror. "Snow White you're not!" said the voice in the mirror.

I took off the dress, put on my clothes, and walked out of the fitting room carrying my hangers of cute clothes. "Which one will it be, the yellow one?" said the annoyingly cute teenager.

"I'm afraid none of them will work for a wedding and an over-30 mother of two."

"Maybe something else would look better on you." She frowned. The frown wasn't quite as contagious as the smile. "You don't look very big to me," she said. "I bet you don't weigh any more than I do."

"I probably don't," I answered. "I still weigh the same; it's just that it has all been redistributed."

She laughed and put away the clothes. I don't think she understood the magnitude of that word *redistributed*.

I think God makes redistribution a fact of life so we don't get too comfortable or too sure of ourselves. Maybe he thinks, "She's doing great in high school. Big fish in a little pond! Time to redistribute." And off we go to college, a little humbled by our new surroundings. Or, "Got a great job? Worked your way to the top of your field, have you? Time to redistribute." Suddenly you're laid off. This'll give you more time to stay home with your children. Or, "Like the way you look? Work hard to look that way, do you? (Bam!) Time to redistribute." You are still the same person, with the same faith in your Savior, and the same talents to share. Only the circumstances have changed. Time to move on.

Enduring redistribution requires faith. God will get you through college. He will find you a new job. He will make you able to take care of those children day after day. Slowly, he will give you acceptance. This redistribution thing requires us to lean on God for the assurance that we are still valuable to him. It forces us to concentrate more on our insides rather than too much on our outsides.

In the end I found an appropriate dress—I looked nice enough. I looked like the mother of the flower girl and the ring bearer. My husband was kind enough to tell me I looked wonderful. Life is good. There are blessings to be found even in redistribution.

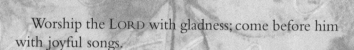

Worship the LORD with gladness; come before him with joyful songs.

Psalm 100:2

Though you have not seen him, you love him; and even though you do not see him now, you believe in him and are filled with an inexpressible and glorious joy.

1 Peter 1:8

Joyful Noise

I was sitting in a pew, putting together the three pieces of my flute, husband and child beside me, another child asleep on the floor in front of me. A wonderful Reformation sermon was drawing to a close, and I was preparing to play a duet with a friend during the offering. I had told her when practice had begun that I didn't usually feel nervous when playing in church. This time, however, the congregation was filled with excellent musicians—including my friend, who is always supportive and helpful, but nevertheless intimidating. I suddenly felt alone. I rose, aware that all eyes were on me, walked to the front of the church, and raised my flute to my lips.

As the music began, so did my shaking. The shaking in my arms was uncontrollable. In a flash I was reliving an incident in the high school band room—a dreaded place of unrelenting stress.

I am a second-chair flautist, supposedly one of the best. We are practicing a symphonic piece. "Someone is playing the wrong note" comes the director's acid critique. Can't be me; I'm doing it right. Over and over again we play that same section, always with the same result. Finally, the director decides to smoke out the wrong note. Beginning at the other end of the flute section, we play the same phrase, one by one. "Toot," right note. "Toot," right note. On and on, until it is my turn. "Toot." Wrong note. I'm the culprit! How can that be? I've been reading music for years. I know the notes. At this point I try very hard not to cry, but the tears puddle up anyway. Suddenly, I can't see a thing. I sit and stare blindly. There is no music; there are no notes; there is no one else in the room. When I can finally see again, I leave the stage until practice is over. Two optometrist appointments later it is concluded that my eyes are fine, but my stress level is way too high.

Later I have been assigned a piccolo solo. I am excited. It is a fun number titled "The Irish Washerwoman." But I don't know we are going to practice the routine already tonight on the field with the entire band listening. I have no music—we are supposed to memorize everything. I haven't memorized my solo yet. I play miserably. I begin to shiver, freezing cold in the autumn night air. The solo becomes a duet. I end up playing the duet well with my best friend. I'm okay but ashamed.

Those incidents flash through my mind as I continue to play in church, counting 1, 2, 3; 1, 2, 3; 1, 2, 3. Somehow, I stay on the beat and most of the notes come out right. The shaking in my arms subsides. It is a beautiful piece of music. It is a quiet, peaceful song of thankfulness amid the loud trumpeting celebrations of the Reformation. When I get a little off in the timing, I leave out one note and listen to my partner. She brings me back, and no one is the wiser. We continue, our flutes moving beside us in the air like floating fall leaves. And then it is over. I pause to let the music resonate, then lower my arms that are no longer shaking, knowing the "performance" could have been better. Yet, there is no stress—only joy.

There is only joy.

There is so much joy that I float through the rest of the evening—the spaghetti dinner—washing all 175 plates, forks, knives, and spoons; singing hymns with the other women as we work. People pass by the kitchen window on their way home and say they enjoyed my music. It is nice to hear.

It is even nicer to hear my heavenly Father's voice saying, "I love you. I love you even when you are the only person in the band playing the wrong note."

I thank God for the talent that I have and for opportunities to use that limited talent to praise and glorify him. I thank God that my Savior's love for me transcends all weakness. The world always asks me to do my best, but I never feel good enough. For God, I want to give my best out of love for him and all he has done for me. Because of Jesus, my best is good enough. My music reaches the ears of God, and he likes it.

I look forward to my next opportunity to play my flute in church. Maybe next time I won't be as nervous, and my arms won't shake, but even then I may not get all the notes right. No matter—I know there will be joy. There will be joy.

Cast all your anxiety on him because he cares for you.

1 Peter 5:7

Do not be anxious about anything, but in everything, by prayer and petition, with thanksgiving, present your requests to God. And the peace of God, which transcends all understanding, will guard your hearts and your minds in Christ Jesus.

Philippians 4:6,7

The Neighbor's Dog

It happened at a birthday party. The neighborhood was gathered, as were friends and relatives, to celebrate the fifth birthday of our neighbor's son. Their dog was chained in the side yard so as not to frighten or annoy guests. We ate and laughed and talked. The children jumped in a huge bouncing castle. All was well until someone went into the front yard. There she was—the beautiful dog who had tried to jump all over us just a few hours before. Dead. She had tried to jump over the fence and had hanged herself on the chain. The adults at the party were saddened, but all kept dry eyes and smiles. No one wanted to spoil the day. The dog's body was removed from the fence and taken to a neighbor's garage until something could be done with it the next day.

That was Sunday afternoon. On Monday our now five-year-old neighbor boy came over to play with our son, as was his habit. I looked at his face. He was smiling, showing no sign of tears or sadness. There was no mention of the dog. I let the boys play and said nothing about the unfortunate accident.

Then our buddy went away to school for a few hours. When he knocked on the door in the afternoon, his face had changed. Before he said anything, I knew that his parents had broken the sad news to him. I hugged him, and I began to cry even before he told us, "My doggie died." He accepted my comfort with grace beyond his years and said, "Can we just play a quiet game today?" And just like that the two boys disappeared into my son's room.

I had waited nearly 24 hours to tell my son what had happened. I wanted him to be prepared to offer comfort to a sad little boy. It had seemed like a very long wait.

This waiting made me think about how much God waits for us. He tells us to talk to him. He gives us the privilege of prayer. He knows when our dog dies, when a friend hurts our feelings, or when things go wrong at work. He waits for us to bring these concerns to him so that he can shoulder the burden with us.

Jesus knows the pain of rejection and of loss. He's been there; he knows how painful life can be; he's experienced it all himself. He is able to dry our tears. But too often we make him wait for us, instead of the other way around. We try to keep the secrets and the heartaches all to ourselves. We can handle them—or so says our sinful pride.

Truth is, God already knows all about our weary struggles. He is willing and ready to give us whatever we need. "Do you need more of my strength? Here, take some from my Word," he says. "There's a never-ending supply." "Do you need a little extra reassurance regarding the promises I've made to you?" Bam. "Listen again to the things I've already done for you." "Feeling empty or lonely or ashamed? I've got just the right thing—my Word of truth and hope."

I prayed then, just to let my Lord Jesus know how I was feeling. He already knew, of course. But I told him anyway—to remind me that he is the source of all good things, of life itself. Besides, I just wanted him to know that it felt good to be able to share this sad burden with him.

I also resolved not to get a dog anytime soon.

Do not worry about tomorrow, for tomorrow will worry about itself. Each day has enough trouble of its own.

Matthew 6:34

Is not wisdom found among the aged? Does not long life bring understanding?

To God belong wisdom and power; counsel and understanding are his.

Job 12:12,13

Getting Old Fast

I am getting old! I am getting *very* old! It is all the fault of my children. I heard it on a television talk show. Compared to women in all other jobs, the highest rate of mortality occurs among stay-at-home moms. It seems there is so much stress and so little recognition that it's taking years off my life. That little tidbit of information gave me just the excuse I needed to be grumpy and lazy and to blame those little monsters for every problem I had.

For days after hearing that comment, my attitude was less than exemplary. I told my kids, "You're driving me crazy!" I complained, "I don't want to hold you right now. My back hurts." I whined, "My brain is turning to mush. Do I have to read another picture book?"

My ears finally got sick and tired of hearing my mouth complain. "Stop whining," they whined. So I did. When I finally did shut up about all the physical punishment and emotional abuse moms have to endure, I realized what a really good parenting model God had placed right in front of my eyes in my lifelong partner.

My husband is a good dad. His schedule is pretty full, but it isn't always terrible. Sometimes he has a minute to play with our children. And play they do. The interesting part was that he didn't seem to be getting any older—he was wrestling and teasing, often acting like a kid himself. At the same time that I was being a grump, he was playing Monopoly in his ten free minutes or reading another story to his daughter. He was taking advantage of the minutes he had, while I was dreading the hours of entrapment.

Sometimes it feels like life is slipping away—that we aren't fulfilling our dreams. Our answer so often is to hurry up, to skip the insignificant details of life, and to get on with chasing our dreams. Do we even stop to ask ourselves if we are going where God wants us to go?

Television is full of images touting ways in which you can live the life of your dreams, telling you that you can't be happy if you don't follow your heart. They never tell us just how self-centered and stupid our hearts can be. We miss so much of the joy of life when we dread the day-to-day moments. We lose out on so many blessings when we abhor those precious times when we seem to be going nowhere.

How many wrinkles do we add to our faces just by worrying about the years?

After the whining I was still stressed by my children, but I began to learn to cope with—and even appreciate—the stress.

Truth be told, I am getting older. But with age comes peace. If motherhood takes years off my life, well then, I guess I will just be with Jesus sooner.

Thanks be to God that, though you used to be slaves to sin, you wholeheartedly obeyed the form of teaching to which you were entrusted. You have been set free from sin and have become slaves to righteousness.

Romans 6:17,18

I myself in my mind am a slave to God's law, but in the sinful nature a slave to the law of sin.

Romans 7:25

Captivated by Christ

One Sunday afternoon after a really busy week, we had collapsed on the sofa and were watching a football game on TV. The children were playing outside, still in their church clothes. My husband and I ate all the junk food we could find in the house, piling up empty wrappers and packages on the living room floor like slobs. It was an exciting game with numerous turnovers, near misses, great catches, and broken tackles. We cheered a little. We booed a little. We snoozed a little, in spite of the excitement. All in all it was a great Sunday afternoon. Near the end of the game, one of the announcers commented on what a "captivating" game it had been. My husband asked if I had been held captive, and I replied, "Only by this couch."

That wasn't quite true. I have been held captive without even thinking about it. I am always captivated by Christ, held tightly in his love.

We are all captives of something. We were once captives of sin. What a dead end kind of captivity! Then the Holy Spirit gave us faith, and we became captivated by Christ. This captivity brings us the freedom to relax and be at peace with ourselves, with our God, and with the people around us. As captives of Christ's love, we desire to serve only him.

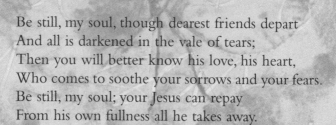

Be still, my soul, though dearest friends depart
And all is darkened in the vale of tears;
Then you will better know his love, his heart,
Who comes to soothe your sorrows and your fears.
Be still, my soul; your Jesus can repay
From his own fullness all he takes away.

CW 415:3

My comfort in my suffering is this: Your promise
preserves my life.

Psalm 119:50

Jan

A rainy day in January,
And I remember Jan.
I see her face the way it was in sixth grade,
Pale but strong,
Her cheeks like fortress walls
Protecting the opulent brown treasures of her eyes.

I remember her hair,
Brown with touches of amber,
The way it was in eleventh grade,
Hanging in curls to her waist,
Like a medieval princess.

I remember her open smile
When she said she had been named after January,
The month of her birth.
I didn't know then
That it would also be the month of her death.

When January threatens to smother me
With its gloomy skies and crying eyes,
I hide behind fortress walls
And think of her.
I remember that she always liked the rain.

Every January I remember the day,
The endless rain,
The pictures of the crash.
I ask God why he took her away.
I always ask.
He always answers.

God gave me a January princess
Who would be my friend.
He climbed the walls of my fortress
And introduced me to a treasure
I will cherish all of my life.

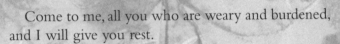

Come to me, all you who are weary and burdened, and I will give you rest.

Matthew 11:28

I am the Alpha and the Omega, the Beginning and the End. To him who is thirsty I will give to drink without cost from the spring of the water of life. He who overcomes will inherit all this, and I will be his God and he will be my son.

Revelation 21:6,7

Rest

On Christmas night we drove home from visiting friends. It had been an enjoyable afternoon and evening—the end to a busy, but happy, holiday. Both children were sleeping in the car. Turning a corner I noticed the moon. It was huge, almost egg shaped, and bright. It seemed to be sitting on a hilltop, resting from its life of orbiting.

I wanted nothing more at that moment than to sit down on the top of my little hill and rest like that moon. I wanted to get home, put the children to bed, and have a shower, a moment to do housework, a little time to read—all by myself.

It didn't happen. What happened was that my daughter woke up and got sick. She threw up and threw up and threw up. I held her, changed her clothes, did laundry, cleaned up, and held her again—over and over and over. Although there was no time for housework or book reading, my husband was able to take over long enough for me to get that now badly needed shower. I got just a moment's rest—for my body and my mind. Just a tiny moment.

But I appreciated that moment, and during this time I thought a bit about rest. Even when there are long hours away from responsibilities, I can never rest from being who I am. I am the mother of two, the wife of one, a friend to many, and a redeemed child of God. Thank God that there is no rest from those blessings.

The moon may have looked as though it were resting on that hill, but the moon is what it is. It will go on orbiting the earth as long as the almighty God ordains it. It cannot rest from being what it is.

After six days of creation, God rested from his creative work. He sat back and looked at what he had created, but he never rested from being who he is. He has never rested from loving us. He has never rested from being perfect and just and powerful and kind. He is always the same. He is always God. He is always there to hold us when we are sick or tired, to clean up our lives for us when we get messy, and to give us perfect rest.

You prepare a table before me in the presence of my enemies. You anoint my head with oil; my cup overflows. Surely goodness and love will follow me all the days of my life, and I will dwell in the house of the LORD forever.

Psalm 23:5,6

Then will the eyes of the blind be opened and the ears of the deaf unstopped. Then will the lame leap like a deer, and the mute tongue shout for joy. Water will gush forth in the wilderness and streams in the desert.

Isaiah 35:5,6

Handicupped

We pulled into the parking lot of our church. As we rolled to a stop, my daughter noticed the wheelchair symbol on the asphalt in the parking space next to ours. Like a reading primer, the symbol led her eyes to the sign that marked the same space. Thinking we were parking in the handicapped spot and not quite knowing the correct word, she asked, "Mom, are we *handicupped*?"

"Well," I answered, "perhaps we are handicupped." She didn't have a clue what I meant, but once again she had said something that made me think about God's love for us.

We used to be handi*capped,* disabled by our sins. We couldn't walk in the way of the Lord. We couldn't jump for joy at the sound of his name. We couldn't make our way into his glorious presence.

Now we are handi*cupped,* and life is so much better. Jesus took away our infirmities and made us capable of being cups— ready to be filled with his joy and blessings, ready to be poured out once again in his service.

Some of our family's favorite Bible stories are those in which we hear of Jesus or his disciples healing someone's handicap, so he or she can become handicupped. When four men brought a paralytic to see Jesus, they had to lower their friend through the roof on a mat. Jesus announced to the man that his sins were forgiven, and then made him walk. We are told, "This amazed everyone and they praised God, saying, 'We have never seen anything like this!'" (Mark 2:12).

When a crippled man asked Peter and James for money, Peter didn't give him money. Instead, Peter gave him the power of God; Peter healed him in the name of Jesus. Like that man, our handicaps are turned upside down. Our hearts are able to leap because we too are filled to overflowing with God's love.

If we have food and clothing, we will be content with that.

1 Timothy 6:8

Here is the bread that comes down from heaven, which a man may eat and not die. I am the living bread that came down from heaven. If anyone eats of this bread, he will live forever. This bread is my flesh, which I will give for the life of the world.

John 6:50,51

Empty Plates

Dinner was over—every plate and bowl on the table was empty. All the food was in the stomachs of my family, and I was a happy woman. I suppose people who don't always get enough to eat may not like the sight of empty plates, but I think most moms in America do. It really isn't much fun to spend time in the kitchen preparing a meal and then have your children say, "I don't like this." It's annoying to wrap up stuff that you know will not taste good tomorrow but, at the same time, would be a waste if thrown out. So all those empty plates and bowls made me smile. My family had happily enjoyed the meal I had slaved over all afternoon. It boosted my ego.

I think God is happy too when we enjoy what he gives—when we consume his blessings with gusto. How sad it must make God when we turn up our noses at the things he offers us and say, "That isn't what I wanted." He fills our plates with good things. He fills our lives with things that may not be our favorites but are spiritually nutritious. He prepares the meals that will help us grow and mature into healthy children of God.

I tell my children to think about how much I love them when I ask them to eat their vegetables. I feed them well because I love them. God feeds us well because he loves us.

I have decided to do a better job of emptying my plate. I have decided to ask God to help me enjoy his blessings—along with the "vegetables" I don't always like. I read his Word to remind me that he gives me what I need because he loves me.

Who of you by worrying can add a single hour to his life?

Matthew 6:27

Then I realized that it is good and proper for a man to eat and drink, and to find satisfaction in his toilsome labor under the sun during the few days of life God has given him—for this is his lot. Moreover, when God gives any man wealth and possessions, and enables him to enjoy them, to accept his lot and be happy in his work—this is a gift of God. He seldom reflects on the days of his life, because God keeps him occupied with gladness of heart.

Ecclesiastes 5:18-20

Surprise

I really thought my 35th birthday would be scary, fraught with dangerous mirrors—showing off my every wrinkle and gray hair. I expected to feel old, depressed, and decrepit. To my surprise it turned out to be an uplifting day, full of beauty and warmth.

I had been invited to have lunch with a friend. She even called to arrange for my husband to be home to watch the children. I didn't know where we were going, but I donned my favorite blouse just because it was my favorite—and it was my birthday. The blouse has my favorite painting on it, *The Lady of Shallott*. When I wear it I match my living room wall. I always feel fun and romantic in it.

When my friend and I arrived at the restaurant, I discovered that the little lunch was a surprise tea party, attended by many friends of all ilks and ages. I cried a little; I laughed a lot. We all tried on hats and sampled delicacies; shared one another's teas and posed for photographs. The atmosphere was graceful and pretty, just like the Lady of Shallott. The smiles were happy; the conversations were interesting and meaningful. I couldn't have asked for a better time.

At home that night, we had planned to have two couples I had never met come over to play board games. This is our way of getting to know prospective members for our church. We had scheduled the evening a few days earlier. Sometimes these evening gatherings can be boring; other times they can be really fun events. I have to admit that on this occasion I was not excited about spending the rest of what had been an otherwise perfect day with strangers. I had had enough grand surprises for one day, but I went through with the plan anyway.

Surprise! The two couples turned out to be wonderful people, and my husband was a pleasant host. How could all these good things happen on a day when I had expected the worst?

I supposed it must have been God's idea all along. The best I could do was to thank him for giving me life and for making my days happy, even when I was doing my best to make them unhappy.

That day taught me a lesson too. In the future I will be more positive about all the surprises that occur every day in life. Maybe then God won't always have to bop me over the head with happiness. No matter how good or bad the surprises may turn out, I am praying that God will help me let him decide how he wants to bless me each new day. In this way I will still be filled with the joy of living every day to his glory.

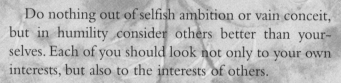

Do nothing out of selfish ambition or vain conceit, but in humility consider others better than yourselves. Each of you should look not only to your own interests, but also to the interests of others.

Philippians 2:3,4

A gift opens the way for the giver and ushers him into the presence of the great.

Proverbs 18:16

Pampered

For my birthday I got a gift certificate to a day spa. It's a neat place, but expensive—one of those places where they do body wraps, facials, manicures, and the like. Other women encouraged me to go and "get pampered." They told me I deserved a few hours off from being wife, mother, and housekeeper. The men who knew about the gift just looked at me as if they couldn't quite figure out what was so great about a facial. I basically ignored the men and listened to the women.

At the spa I was struck by the exquisite aromas, oils, and lotions. My facial, manicure, and pedicure were delightful. I loved every moment of each.

As I was lying in a darkened room, listening to delicate music and letting the facial mask work its magic, I thought about the whole idea of being pampered. Do we really need to be pampered? Is spoiling ourselves good? Should I have felt guilty about my pleasure? I thought about a daytime talk show I had seen recently. It was all about the strange things people do to be alone in order to find out who they really are. One man left his family for six months—with their approval. They claimed, upon his return, that the experience had made him a better husband and father. Another woman camped out in the desert for 30 days. One young man chose not to speak for one entire year. There were stories too of women who felt they had lost their true selves as a result of marriage and motherhood. These women were encouraged to get away, to do the things that made them happy. They were told that their families would be stronger and healthier if Mom made herself happy—through pampering or a job or time away from home.

I have to admit, I enjoyed my two hours of leisure. I might even do it again in a year or two. But I also decided that it wasn't necessary. I'm sure God wants us to be happy and to have blessings that make us feel special and loved. I'm also sure that I do not need to go off and find myself—in solitude or in being pampered. I am myself where God has put me. I am his child wherever I go. The roles I play in my life are blessings from him.

I have decided to spend some of my time alone with God. I need to study his Word. I need to pray. I need to let him speak to me. I must not, however, be fooled by the notion that if I give too much of myself to others, I will lose my personal identity. Giving God's love away only makes me happier; being his servant makes me more of who I am. An occasional day of pampering is an added blessing—not necessary, just nice.

Trust in the LORD with all your heart and lean not on your own understanding; in all your ways acknowledge him, and he will make your paths straight.

Proverbs 3:5,6

You may say to yourself, "My power and the strength of my hands have produced this wealth for me." But remember the LORD your God, for it is he who gives you the ability to produce wealth, and so confirms his covenant, which he swore to your forefathers, as it is today.

Deuteronomy 8:17,18

What Brings the Future?

The time had finally come when my two children were getting older and more independent. I was beginning to realize that I could leave the house for a few hours a day and feel good about it. I wanted to contribute some income to my household. I wanted to use my adult brain. Although more children may be waiting in the future, I was happy to be out of the rewarding, yet grueling, infant and toddler years, at least for a while.

I started looking for jobs. I read the classifieds in the newspaper. I scanned the Internet. I talked to people about jobs. I filled out applications, talked to potential employers, and mulled over the pros and cons of numerous jobs. The jobs that paid enough to cover day care and to supplement our bank account required too much of my time and my effort. I still wanted to be with my children many hours of the day. I wondered if the job I wanted existed at all.

I went for an interview, not sure even as I sold myself to the "search committee" that the job was right for me. Then something very strange happened. The group of women interviewing me told me I was overqualified. I knew that, but I wanted a part-time job. They said they were going to do a little career counseling, and before I had time to leave the building, I had set up another interview. The new job they offered paid three times as much as the one for which I had interviewed, and the hours were better. It was the perfect job for me. I got the job even before I applied for it.

My first thought was "This has to be divine intervention. What else could it be?" The job fell into my lap, a baby-sitter fell into my lap, and a wise woman who was retiring from the position taught me what to do quickly and thoroughly. God was truly in control.

We all know that God is in control. We all know that he knows what is best for us and gives us beautiful blessings. The Bible tells us not to worry. But as many times as we try to internalize the promise, sometimes we still worry. The longer we live as Christians, the more times we see God's hand at work in our lives, the more we start to look for his power. The more power we see, the calmer we become. We worry less— we trust God more, because we have seen what he can do.

I have seen what he can do. I have seen him work things out in my life in so many ways.

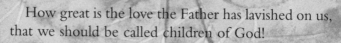

How great is the love the Father has lavished on us, that we should be called children of God!

1 John 3:1

As a mother comforts her child, so will I comfort you.

Isaiah 66:13

Awakening

I was a child cradling my dolly,
Sleep-walking,
Afraid of my dreams.

His music awakened me.

I am a child believing in Jesus,
Faith-walking,
Following my dreams.

His music soothes me.

I am a child praising Jesus,
Joy-walking,
Enjoying my dreams.

His music delights me.

I am a child trusting Jesus,
Love-walking,
Heaven is my dream.

His music is life to me.

Sweet the moments, rich in blessing,
Which before the cross we spend,
Life and health and peace possessing
From the sinner's dying friend.

Lord, in loving contemplation
Fix our hearts and eyes on you
Till we taste your full salvation
And your unveiled glory view.

CW 111:1,5

Afterword

The moments of our lives are many and varied, full of emotion and rich with growth. There are moments of fear and courage, moments of sadness and joy, moments that consist of both the mundane and the exotic, moments alone and moments to be shared. Every second of our lives is a gift from God; every day, another opportunity to praise him. Each event leads us into a closer relationship with our Lord, making every moment one that is sweet and precious.

So many times in my life, I have felt weak, foolish, or insignificant. It has been helpful during those times to play my little game, to ask myself, "What is the spiritual significance of this moment?" Often the game leads me to a search of Scripture, and Scripture strengthens my faith. It is there that God reminds me that his grace is sufficient—that his power is made perfect in my weakness. It is there that I am told: "God chose the foolish things of the world to shame the wise; God chose the weak things of the world to shame the strong. He chose the lowly things of this world and the despised things—and the things that are not—to nullify the things that are, so that no one may boast before him. It is because of him that [I am] in Christ Jesus, who has become for us wisdom from God—that is our righteousness, holiness and redemption. Therefore, as it is written: 'Let him who boasts boast in the Lord'" (1 Corinthians 1:27-31). The game I play leads me to boast in the Lord; it teaches me to rely on Jesus as my strength and my wisdom.

There are also those precious moments that are filled with observable blessings. Such moments give us renewed confidence, added strength, and joy for the long journey that is life. During these times I still play the game. I ask myself, "What is God trying to tell me about himself? Is this a taste of heaven?" There is great beauty in these moments because they are always anchored in God's sure promises. I give thanks for them and appreciate them. That is all that I can do.

Some moments are mundane and trivial. In these times I ask myself, "What reasons does God have for putting me into this situation?" There are those times when I am unable to discern an answer, but I usually discover that such moments aren't really trivial at all. God has a purpose, even if I may not always understand what it might be. Nothing about God or his relationship with me is mundane. In the end, Jesus makes every moment a significant moment. Having him at my side makes every tick of the clock a sweet moment.